NATURAL SWEETS

A mouth-watering selection of wholefood recipes for making your own confectionery.

NATURAL SWEETS

by

Janet Hunt

Illustrated by Clive Birch

THORSONS PUBLISHERS LIMITED
Wellingborough, Northamptonshire

First published 1984

British Library Cataloguing in Publication Data

Hunt, Janet, 1942-
    Natural sweets.
    1 Candy   2. Cookery (Natural foods)
    I. Title
    641.8'53   TX791

    ISBN 0-7225-0913-8

Reproduced, printed and bound in Great Britain by
Hazell Watson & Viney Limited,
Member of the BPCC Group,
Aylesbury, Bucks

CONTENTS

	Page
Introduction	7
Traditional Confectionery	13
Sweets from Around the World	28
Wholesome and Delicious	44
Nibblers' Delights	58
Index	63

INTRODUCTION

Ask anyone what they think about sweets, and they'll probably admit, if somewhat reluctantly, that they're bad for health, teeth and tummy bulge. This awareness, however, doesn't stop the British leading the world in the consumption of confectionery — it simply detracts from the pleasure of eating sweet things by adding a feeling of guilt.

Yet it wasn't so long ago that sweets were attributed to have a number of nutritional benefits. Marshmallows, made from an extract of the roots of the marshmallow plant, were considered to be an excellent medicine for chest ailments. Honey, the first known sweetener (Stone Age man, it seems, had a sweet tooth too!), has long been reputed to help relieve insomnia, indigestion, and a variety of other ailments. Chocolate, it was thought, should be eaten regularly in the cause of robust health.

The notoriety of sweets today may well stem from the fact that they are no longer made from natural ingredients. Produced in factories on a vast scale they are coloured, flavoured and over-sweetened to tempt today's dulled palates; are treated so that they stay edible for months if not years; are advertised as 'full of goodness' and 'less fattening'. Most of the bars and bags you'll find in your local sweets shop are full of fats and empty calories whilst being virtually devoid of nutrition. No doubt about it — sweets deserve their reputation.

And still, contradictorily, we continue to see them as something special, a treat, a comfort, a placebo. Birthdays,

Mother's Day, anniversaries, Easter, Christmas — all ar
occasions traditionally celebrated with sweets. Whe
someone is in need of cheering up, when boy courts girl, whe
we go to the theatre or cinema, sweets again come instantl
to mind.

Many wholefooders condemn sweets out of hand. But i
this fair? And — more important — is it logical? Our lov
of sweet foods is a very natural one; most babies prefer swee
tastes to savoury (which is why so many baby foods are ful
of sugar, even those that are based on savoury ingredients!)
If sweet things are important to us, as obviously they are
it seems foolish to forbid them. Much wiser, surely to fin
a way to put nutrition back into them so that instead of bein;
harmful, they are a good source of wholesome nourishment
just like they used to be.

The best way to do this is, of course, to make them yoursel
— which is what this book aims to help you do. In it you'
find recipes for family favourites such as fondants, fudge an
nougat; for sweets that are popular in other parts of th
world, where cooks still use more traditional methods, anc
ingredients such as honey, nuts and seeds; some simple sweet
made with little or no sugar, that rely on fruits for their swee
flavour; and last of all — a few ideas for nibblers. Some o
the recipes can be thrown together in minutes, others are
much longer and more complicated, requiring patience anc
possibly one or two items of equipment. Whichever you
decide to tackle, make the making of the sweets as much a
part of the pleasure as the eating — maybe share it with a
friend, or a younger member of the family. Eat them whilst
they are fresh as few of them will keep for long (or give them

8

s a gift — home-made sweets are so much more welcome
than the factory-made variety!).

Most important of all, think of them as something special,
an occasional treat rather than a daily food, just as they used
to be in fact. That way you'll consume less sugar and calories,
and derive far more pleasure from a taste to which you are
not TOO accustomed!

BEFORE YOU START

Most of the recipes given here use only natural ingredients,
though a few of them contain such things as liquid glucose,
bicarbonate of soda, etc. The reason is that these additives
are necessary to get a certain finish, texture, whatever. If you
prefer not to use such ingredients, try one of the many recipes
that *are* completely free of additives. When choosing which
raw cane sugar to use, remember that the end product will
look as dark as the variety you use. For more traditional
sweets use the very light raw cane sugar that is now available.
Additional colourings are best kept to a minimum — they
really aren't necessary. But if you do want to use them, try
concentrated fruit juice for red, orange, black, yellow; coffee
for browns; a tiny amount of spinach for green. When buying
flavouring, remember that extracts and essences are more
likely to come from natural sources than anything labelled
'flavouring'.

The more traditional recipes are the ones that also require
more specialized equipment. Always use a heavy based
saucepan when making a syrup (and make sure the sugar has
dissolved completely before you bring it to the boil). Make

9

sure your wooden spoons and spatulas have long handles t
avoid splashing yourself with boiling syrup. A suga
thermometer will help enormously, and is especially usef
if you intend to do a lot of sweet-making. If not, howeve
you can judge the various stages your syrup has reached b
dropping a teaspoonful of the syrup into a cup of cold wate
and noting its reaction. (Always remove the saucepan fro
the heat whilst you do this.) These are the stages throug
which the syrup will go:

Smooth — 220°F/105°C
Sugar will cling to fingers in a sticky film.

Soft ball — 237°F/114°C
Syrup can be rolled into a soft ball between fingers.

Firm ball — 247°F/119°C
Forms a firm but pliable ball.

Soft crack — 280°F/137°C
Separates into threads which break quite easily.

Hard crack — 310°F/154°C
Separates into hard, brittle threads.

Caramel — 340°F/171°C
Sugar goes much darker.

One last point. Sweet recipes, like all recipes, are not a se
of hard and fast rules. They are guide lines. Once you hav

mastered the art of combining ingredients in the ways suggested, try some new combinations of your own, adjust the proportions, change the flavourings. Have fun. After all, the purpose of confectionery — even the most nutritious kind — is to give pleasure.

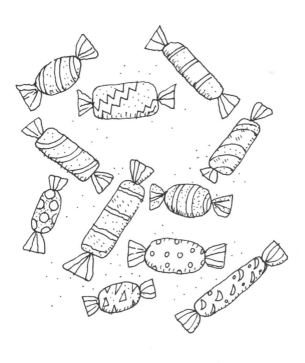

TRADITIONAL CONFECTIONERY

PRESERVED GINGER TABLET

1 lb (455g) raw cane sugar
¼ pint (140ml) water
1 teaspoonful ground ginger
2 tablespoonsful preserved ginger, chopped
  finely

1. In a saucepan combine the sugar, water and ground ginger, and cook, stirring, until it comes to the boil. Continue boiling gently for about 10 minutes, until the mixture reaches soft ball stage (temperature 237°F/114°C).

2. Off the heat, continue stirring so that the mixture becomes creamy and thick. Add the chopped ginger.

3. Pour into a lightly greased shallow tin and leave to cool for a few minutes, then mark into squares. When cold, break to separate the squares.

YOGURT WALNUT FUDGE

⅓ pint (200ml) plain yogurt
1 teaspoonful bicarbonate of soda
1 lb (455g) raw cane sugar
1 tablespoonful liquid glucose
2 oz (55g) butter or polyunsaturated
   margarine
3 oz (85g) walnuts, chopped coarsely

1. Put the yogurt into a saucepan and stir in the bicarbonate of soda, then let mixture stand for 30 minutes.

2. Add the sugar and liquid glucose and bring the mixture gently to the boil, stirring continually. Add the butter, making sure it melts completely. Continue boiling steadily, stirring now and again, for approximately 15 minutes until the mixture reaches soft ball stage (temperature 237°F/114°C).

3. Take the saucepan off the heat and leave for 5 minutes. Beat the fudge mixture until it loses its gloss and becomes thick and creamy. Stir in the chopped nuts. Grease a large shallow tin and pour in the mixture. Cut into squares when cool.

HONEY NOYEAU

14 oz (395g) raw cane sugar
¼ pint (140ml) water
3 tablespoonsful liquid glucose
2 tablespoonsful honey
2 oz (55g) almonds
Rice paper

1. In a saucepan combine the sugar and water, and heat gently until the sugar dissolves. Stir in the glucose and continue boiling steadily until the mixture reaches soft ball stage (temperature 237°F/114°C).

2. Pour into a wetted dish and leave to cool for a few minutes. Stir in the warmed honey and continue stirring until you have a thick, creamy paste.

3. Coarsely chop the nuts and add them to the other ingredients, mixing well.

4. Line a shallow tin with the rice paper and spread the mixture over it to a depth of about ½ inch (1cm). Top with more rice paper, a piece of cardboard, and a heavy weight. Leave overnight. Cut into squares to serve.

FONDANT ROLL

2 egg whites
1 lb (455g) raw cane sugar, powdered in grinder
2 oz (55g) unsalted butter
Few drops green food colouring*
Few drops red food colouring*
1 teaspoonful vanilla essence

1. In a bowl beat one of the egg whites until it begins to stiffen. Use a metal spoon to mix in the sugar.

2. Soften the butter and add it to the mixture, beating well so that it becomes light and fluffy.

3. Divide into three equal-sized portions. Mix the green colouring into one, the red into another, and flavour the last portion with the vanilla essence.

4. On a sheet of greaseproof paper, and using a wet rolling-pin or spatula, shape each of the pieces of fondant into rectangles about ¼ in (½cm) thick, and as equal as possible in size.

5. Use a pastry brush to lightly coat the green sheet with a little of the other lightly beaten egg white, and lay the pink sheet on top of it. Brush this with egg white and top with the final sheet of fondant. Press down or roll gently to make the layers stick together.

6. Form the fondant into a Swiss-roll shape, brush the edge with egg white, and press together firmly. Wrap

in greaseproof paper and leave for at least 6 hours, preferably overnight, in the cool. Serve cut crossways into slices.

*See note on flavourings page 9.

PEPPERMINT ICE

1 lb (455g) raw cane sugar
¼ pint (140ml) water
1 teaspoonful peppermint essence

1. In a saucepan combine the sugar and water. Bring slowly to the boil, stirring continually to dissolve the sugar. Then lower the heat, but continue to boil (without stirring) for about 10 minutes. The syrup is ready when it reaches firm ball stage (temperature 247°F/119°C).

2. Remove from the heat immediately and stir in the peppermint essence, making sure it is well distributed through the syrup.

3. Pour into a shallow ready greased tin, smooth the top with a knife, and leave to firm. Cut into squares when cold.

CREAMY CAROB TRUFFLES

2 oz (55g) carob 'chocolate' bar
2 tablespoonful double cream
1 teaspoonful vanilla essence
½ lb (225g) raw cane sugar
Carob powder to coat

1. Break the carob bar into small pieces and put into the top of a double boiler, or a basin over a pan of hot water (do not let it actually touch the water). Cover and leave to melt, stirring occasionally.

2. Remove from the heat and stir in the cream, then the vanilla essence. Work the sugar into the mixture (this is easiest if you first powder it in a grinder), then turn onto a plate and leave until it is cool enough to handle comfortably.

3. Shape into small balls and roll each one lightly in the carob powder. Serve as they are, or briefly chilled for a firmer texture.

Note: If you prefer, use raw sugar chocolate instead of the carob bar. For a sweeter truffle, coat the balls in a mixture of carob powder and finely ground raw cane vanilla sugar.

PENNIES OF GOLD

2 oz (55g) butter or polyunsaturated margarine
2 tablespoonsful honey
2 oz (55g) raw cane sugar
1 teaspoonful concentrated orange juice
2 oz (55g) wholemeal flour

1. Melt the fat and add it to the honey and sugar, mixing well. Stir in the orange juice.

2. Sprinkle in the flour and mix well.

3. Drop small spoonsful of the mixture onto greased baking sheets, leaving a good space between each one, and flattening slightly with a fork. Bake at 325°F/170°C (Gas Mark 3) for 7-10 minutes, or until golden. Cool briefly on the sheet, then transfer to a wire rack and leave to set firm.

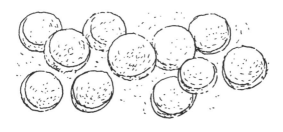

EDINBURGH ROCK

1 lb (455g) raw cane sugar
½ pint (285ml) water
Good pinch cream of tartar
Flavouring of your choice*

1. Put the sugar and water into a saucepan, heat steadily, and stir to dissolve the sugar. Add the cream of tartar and boil the syrup until it reaches firm ball stage (temperature 247°F/119°C).

2. Pour at once onto a cold, hard work surface, preferably a marble slab, and leave a few minutes. As the mixture cools and begins to harden round the edges, use a lightly oiled metal spatula to loosen the sides, and fold them over to the middle. Repeat this until you have a small parcel, then divide it into portions. Add the flavouring, mixing it in well.

3. Now pull the syrup to give it a satiny sheen and open texture. To do this, oil your hands lightly, then shape the mixture into a roll and stretch it out. Fold it up again, and stretch as before, and continue doing so for at least 10 minutes until it becomes creamy and opaque. If it becomes too hard to work, warm it slightly. (A dough hook makes the task much easier.)

4. Pull the rock into sticks, being careful not to twist it. Leave for at least 24 hours, perferably in a warm spot and uncovered. Store in airtight tins or jars.

*Edinburgh rock can be made in a wide variety of colours and flavours. Natural ingredients you can use include fruit juices such as raspberry, lemon, pineapple, orange. You could also add peppermint or almond essence, ground cinnamon or ginger, rose or orange flower water. If you intend to add more than one flavouring to the original rock syrup, get someone to 'pull' each flavour — it's impossible to do the job alone.

EVERTON TOFFEE

4 oz (115g) butter or polyunsaturated margarine
½ lb (225g) raw cane sugar
½ lb (225g) honey or molasses

1. In a saucepan placed over a gentle heat, melt the fat then add the sugar and honey or molasses. Stir until the syrup is thick and smooth.

2. Bring to the boil, and continue boiling steadily, without stirring, until the mixture reaches hard crack stage (temperature 310°F/154°C).

3. Grease a shallow tin, pour in the mixture, and set aside to cool. Mark into squares, and break when completely set. If the toffee is not to be eaten at once, wrap each piece in cellophane to stop it becoming sticky.

COFFEE CREAMS

1 lb (455g) raw cane sugar
1 good tablespoonful coffee powder, or to taste*
2 oz (55g) butter or polyunsturated margarine
2 tablespoonsful milk

1. In a bowl mix together the sugar and coffee powder.

2. Melt the fat and stir in the milk, then add the liquid to the sugar mixture and stir well. On a board, knead the mixture until it is smooth and firm — it it is too soft, add more sugar; if too dry, add a drop more milk.

3. Break the dough into small pieces and roll them into balls, then flatten to make discs. Set aside to firm up.

*You can use instant coffee powder, decaffeinated or dandelion coffee for this recipe. Adjust the amount to suit your taste.

PINEAPPLE FUDGE

½ pint (285ml) milk
1¾ lb (800g) raw cane sugar
4 oz (115g) butter or polyunsaturated margarine
2 teaspoonsful lemon essence
*Approx. 4 oz (115g) fresh or tinned pineapple, well
   drained*

1. Bring the milk slowly to the boil, then add the sugar
   and butter, and continue cooking and stirring until
   the mixture is smooth.

2. Return it to the boil, then cover with a lid and
   continue cooking a few minutes more. Remove the
   lid and boil steadily, stirring occasionally, until the
   mixture reaches soft ball stage (temperature
   237°F/114°C).

3. Take off the heat immediately, stir in the lemon
   essence, and leave the mixture to stand for 5 minutes.
   Now beat until the fudge is thick and creamy. Stir in
   the crushed or chopped pineapple, pour into a
   greased tin, and leave to cool. Mark into squares
   before it sets firm, but do not break until it is
   completely cold.

CHOCOLATE BRAZILS

2 oz (55g) Brazil nuts
Approx. 4 oz (115g) raw sugar chocolate*

1. Make sure the nuts are free of any skin — if this is hard to remove, roast them briefly in the oven so that the skin flakes.

2. Break the chocolate into small pieces and put it into the top of a double boiler, or a bowl suspended over a pan of hot water (making sure it does not touch the water). Cover, and leave to melt, stirring every now and again.

3. Check the consistency of the melted chocolate. If it is too thin, cool briefly; if too thick, heat gently a minute or two more.

4. Using a dipping fork, drop the nuts one at a time into the chocolate, then turn them to make sure they are completely coated. Lift out, tapping the fork against the side of the bowl to remove any excess chocolate.

5. Space the chocolates well apart on a tray lined with greaseproof paper, and allow to set hard before eating.

*Although eating chocolate can be used for this recipe, a more professional finish can be achieved with dipping chocolate, available from trade suppliers and specialists. It is unlikely that a raw sugar version can be bought over the counter.

LEMON LOLLIPOPS

½ lb (225g) raw cane sugar
2 teaspoonsful liquid glucose
6 tablespoonsful lemon juice
Wooden or paper lollipop sticks

1. In a saucepan combine the sugar, glucose and lemon juice. Heat gently, stirring continually, to dissolve the sugar.

2. Bring the mixture to the boil and continue boiling, without stirring, until it reaches hard crack stage (temperature 310°F/154°C). Remove from the heat at once.

3. Using a tablespoon, and working quickly, pour small even-sized discs of the syrup onto a lightly greased baking sheet or other cold surface. When only a little syrup remains, press a stick into each one of the discs, and secure it by pouring a few drops more of the syrup over the top.

4. Leave to cool completely, then lift carefully with a knife or metal spatula. Wrap each lollipop in a cellophane envelope to keep them from softening.

MARZIPAN PETITS FOURS

1 lb (455g) raw cane sugar
¼ pint (140ml) water
¾ lb (340g) ground almonds
2 egg whites
Few drops orange flower water or almond essence
Powdered raw cane sugar
Natural colouring, cloves, etc.

1. Put the sugar and water into saucepan and bring slowly to the boil, stirring continually. Carry on boiling the syrup until it reaches soft ball stage (temperature 237°F/114°C).

2. Remove from the heat and stir lightly for a minute or two. Add the ground almonds, mixing well to make a soft paste. Add the lightly beaten egg whites and cook over a very low heat for a few minutes more. Stir in the essence. Set aside to cool slightly.

3. On a board that has been dusted with powdered sugar, knead the marzipan until it is smooth and pliable. Shape into small fruits, adding colouring as required. Set the *petits fours* aside to firm up.

Note: Ideas for marzipan fruits can include:

Apples — colour them green and use cloves for calyxes.

Oranges — colour orange, add clove, use fine grater to give pitted effect.

Peaches — give them a smooth finish and use a knife to dent one side.

Strawberries — use fine grater to give pitted look.
Berries or grapes — combine a number of tiny balls in a cluster.

ANGUS TOFFEE

1½ lb (680g) raw cane sugar
2 oz (55g) ground almonds
1 oz (30g) butter
¼ pint (140ml) milk

1. Combine all the ingredients in a saucepan, and heat gently whilst stirring continually until the mixture comes to a boil. Continue boiling and stirring over a medium heat for about 7 minutes.

2. Remove from the heat and beat the mixture until it thickens.

3. Pour it into a well greased shallow tin and smooth the top with a knife. Leave to cool, marking into squares before it sets hard. Break into individual pieces when cold.

SWEETS FROM AROUND THE WORLD

NOUGAT (Spain)

1 lb (455g) blanched almonds
1 oz (30g) butter or polyunsaturated margarine
¾ lb (340g) raw cane sugar
Rice paper

1. Chop the almonds into small pieces. Melt the fat in a saucepan and gently fry the almonds until they begin to colour.

2. In a mortar and pestle, pound the nuts with half of the sugar to make a coarse powder, then add the rest of the sugar and mix well.

3. Turn the mixture into a saucepan and cook slowly, stirring frequently, until it thickens.

4. Line a shallow tin with the rice paper, and pour in the mixture, spreading it evenly. Top with more rice paper and press down firmly, then cover with cardboard and a weight. Leave to get completely cold before cutting into squares.

YELLOW MAN (Ireland)

1 oz (30g) butter
½ lb (225g) raw cane sugar
1 dessertspoonful water
1 lb (455g) syrup*
1 teaspoonful bicarbonate of soda

1. In a saucepan melt the butter and spread it over the base. Add the sugar, water and syrup, and bring slowly to the boil, stirring so that the sugar dissolves. Then continue boiling gently, without stirring, until it reaches hard crack stage (temperature 310°F/ 154°C).

2. Add the soda, mixing it in well.

3. Pour the mixture onto a lightly greased cold surface such as a marble slab or a flat dish. As it cools, use a spatula to turn in the edges. When cool enough to handle, roll the syrup up, stretch it, fold, and continue pulling it in this way until it becomes pale. (See Edinburgh Rock page 20.)

4. Break into pieces and leave to set. (Or follow the Irish tradition of leaving it to set in a lump, and break pieces off as required.)

Yellow Man is usually made with syrup, but would be more nutritious — and equally delicious — if made with honey or molasses.

MARRONS GLACÉS (France)

¾ lb (340g) peeled chestnuts
¾ lb (340g) raw cane sugar
1½ tablespoonsful liquid glucose
Bare 4 tablespoonsful water

1. Cook the chestnuts in a saucepan of water for about 30 minutes, or until they are just tender but no overcooked. Drain well.

2. In another pan combine the sugar, glucose and water and cook gently, stirring to dissolve the sugar Continue cooking for a short time until the syrup reaches the smooth stage (temperature 220°F/105°C). Set aside in a bowl to cool, then add the chestnuts, making sure they are covered, and leave to soak for 24 hours.

3. Gradually heat the syrup again, removing the chestnuts just before it begins to boil, then continue cooking until it reaches a temperature just a fraction higher than the stage reached the day before. Remove from the heat, return the chestnuts to the bowl, and leave overnight.

4. Repeat this procedure, but take the temperature of the syrup slightly higher still before you remove it from the heat and return the chestnuts to the bowl Leave overnight.

5. Repeat step 4.

6.   Drain the chestnuts on a wire rack, and leave to dry in a warm spot for at least 24 hours before packing away in an airtight container.

Note: This is the traditional way to make *marrons glacés*, and you really need a sugar thermometer if you are going to make them properly.

CRANBERRY SWEETS (Russia)

1 lb (455g) fresh cranberries *
½ lb (225g) raw cane sugar
1 egg white

1.   Wash and carefully dry the cranberries; powder the sugar in a grinder.

2.   Beat together the sugar and egg white until stiff, then dip the cranberries into the mixture, making sure they are well coated.

3.   Arrange them on a baking sheet and bake at 225°F/110°C (Gas Mark ¼) for about 10 minutes, or until dry.

If you cannot get cranberries, try this recipe using other small berries instead.

TURKISH DELIGHT (Turkey)

¼ teaspoonful tartaric acid
1-2 teaspoonsful rosewater
2 oz (55g) cornflour
1¼ lbs (565g) raw cane sugar
Just over ½ pint (285ml) water
1 oz (30g) pistachio nuts
Powdered raw cane sugar to coat

1. In a bowl combine the tartaric acid, rosewater, and cornflour with just a tiny drop of water to make a paste.

2. In a saucepan combine the sugar and water, and bring gently to the boil, stirring continually. Continue boiling without stirring until the mixture is thick and smooth (temperature 220°F/105°C).

3. Stir the cornflour mixture into the syrup, mixing it thoroughly, then add the coarsely crushed pistachio nuts. Pour into a shallow lightly greased tin and cool.

4. When set, remove the sweet from the tin and cut it into squares, rolling each one in a generous amount of the powdered sugar.

COCONUT BARFI (India)

1 pint (570ml) milk
6 oz (170g) desiccated coconut
3 oz (85g) raw cane sugar
Good pinch ground cardamom
1 tablespoonful rosewater

1. In a saucepan, bring the milk to the boil, then lower the heat and simmer for 10-15 minutes, stirring occasionally to stop it boiling over.

2. Add the coconut and cook for a minute more, then add the sugar, cardamom and rosewater, and cook gently, stirring frequently.

3. When the mixture becomes thick and dry, turn into a shallow lightly greased tin and smooth the top. Leave to get completely cold and firm. Cut into squares.

SUGARED ALMONDS (France)

¾ lb (340g) raw cane sugar
6 tablespoonsful water
1 lb (455g) unblanched almonds

1. In a saucepan heat together the sugar and wate
    stirring so that the sugar dissolves. Boil gently till tl
    mixture reaches soft ball stage (temperatu
    237°F/114°C).

2. Remove from the heat and use a wooden spoon to st
    in the almonds, then continue beating until the syru
    turns powdery. Tip the nuts into a sieve or colande
    and shake well so that the sugar falls through into
    bowl.

3. Return the almond sugar to a saucepan and add ju:
    enough water to cover it. Stir well and cook gentl
    until the syrup clears.

4. Add the nuts, making sure they are all coated wit
    the sugar mixture, then turn the contents of th
    saucepan onto greaseproof paper. Separate th
    almonds and leave to cool.

SESAME CRUNCH (Greece)

½ lb (225g) sesame seeds
2 oz (55g) raw cane sugar
10 oz (285g) honey

1. Put the seeds into a frying pan, spread evenly, and cook gently for 5 minutes, stirring frequently. When they are a pale golden colour, remove from the heat and set aside.

2. In a saucepan combine the seeds, sugar and honey. Bring to the boil and continue boiling slowly for about 15 minutes, until the mixture reaches hard crack stage (temperature 310°F/154°C).

3. Pour onto a greased baking sheet or metal tray and spread thinly. Mark into squares with a knife. When cool, cut or break into individual pieces.

PINE NUT SWEETS (Italy)

5 oz (140g) pine nuts
¾ lb (340g) raw cane sugar
¼ pint (140ml) water
2 tablespoonsful grated lemon peel

1. Gently roast the nuts in a frying pan, or a medium oven, for a few minutes only, taking care they do no colour.

2. In a saucepan combine the sugar and water, stir, an cook slowly until the sugar dissolves completely Bring syrup to the boil and continue cooking until reaches hard crack stage (temperature 310°F/154°C Remove from the heat at once.

3. Stir in the nuts and grated lemon peel, and drop sma spoonsful of the mixture onto a baking sheet covere with greased foil. Leave to cool completely.

CANDIED LIME PEEL (Mexico)

6 limes
¾ lb (340g) raw cane sugar
Extra sugar for coating

1. Peel the fruit carefully with a sharp knife, discarding any of the white pith that may be attached to the skin. Cut into small thin strips.

2. In a saucepan, cover the peel with cold water, bring slowly to the boil, and simmer for a few minutes, then drain well. Cover with more water, bring to the boil as before, then drain the peel. Repeat this process 3 or 4 times (to remove any bitter taste).

3. Return the peel to the saucepan, add the sugar, and a spoonful or two of water — just enough to cover the other ingredients. Heat gently and stir to dissolve the sugar, then cook slowly, with the pan partially covered, for about 40 minutes. The peel is ready when it becomes translucent.

4. Arrange peel on a sheet of greaseproof paper and cool slightly. Toss in the extra sugar. Now leave on the paper, or on a wire rack, until completely dry. Store in an airtight container and use as a nibble, or chopped and added to other confectionery, baked goods, desserts or ice creams.

NOUGAT WITH NUTS
AND HONEY (Italy)

Rice paper
1 lb (455g) broken hazelnuts, lightly roasted
½ lb (225g) raw cane sugar
1 teaspoonful lemon rind, finely grated
½ teaspoonful ground cinnamon
Just under ¼ pint (140ml) runny honey
2 egg whites

1. Line a shallow tin, approximately 8 in. (20cm) square, with rice paper. Chop or crush the nuts and mix with the sugar, lemon rind and cinnamon.

2. In a saucepan gently heat the honey, add the nut and sugar mixture, and stir to make sure the sugar dissolves. Bring slowly to the boil and continue cooking until the mixture reaches soft crack stage (temperature 280°F/ 137°C).

3. Remove from the heat immediately and quickly fold in the stiffly beaten egg whites. Pour the mixture into the prepared tin and cover with more rice paper. Leave to cool completely before cutting into small squares.

PISTACHIO LADUS (India)

4 tablespoonsful ghee*
4 oz (115g) gram flour
6 oz (170g) raw cane sugar
1 oz (30g) pistachio nuts
Pinch ground cardamom (optional)

1. Melt the ghee and stir in the flour, making sure there are no lumps. Continue cooking gently, stirring frequently, for about 10 minutes when the flour will begin to colour.

2. Off the heat add the sugar, chopped nuts and cardamom, and stir well to dissolve the sugar. Set aside to cool for a short while.

3. Whilst the mixture is still soft enough to mould, shape it into small balls. Allow to harden completely before serving.

*If you cannot get hold of ghee (a clarified butter much used in Indian cookery), use butter instead.

MAPLE PECAN FONDANTS (America)

⅓ pint (200ml) pure maple syrup
1 lb 2 oz (500g) raw cane sugar
4 tablespoonsful water
⅛ teaspoonful cream of tartar
2 oz (55g) pecan nut halves

1. Combine the syrup, sugar and water in a saucepan and bring gently to the boil, stirring so that the sugar dissolves. Add the cream of tartar.

2. Continue boiling the syrup over a medium heat for about 10 minutes until it reaches soft ball stage (temperature 237°F/114°C). Brush down the sides of the saucepan to stop crystals forming.

3. Pour the syrup into a large dish or baking tray sprinkled with water, and leave to cool for a short time. When a skin forms over the surface, work the fondant quickly with a spoon or spatula until it has a creamy, grained texture. When cool enough to handle, knead the fondant to make it soft and smooth.

4. Sprinkle a plate with water, mould the fondant into a ball, and put it onto the plate covered with a damp cloth. Leave to ripen for 6-12 hours in a cool place or fridge.

5. Put the fondant into the top of a double boiler, or a basin standing over a pan of hot water, and melt it

very gently, stirring continually with a wooden spoon. If it is too thick, add a tiny drop of water. Do not overheat.

6. Fill small individual cases with the mixture and press a pecan half on top of each one. Leave to cool completely before serving.

PEANUT BRITTLE (West Africa)

1 lb (455g) peanuts
½ lb (225g) raw cane sugar
½ pint (285ml) water
1 teaspoonful lemon juice

1. Spread the nuts on a baking sheet and cook them
    gently in the oven until they begin to colour. Cool,
    then remove the skins.

2. In a saucepan combine the sugar and water, and cook
    over a medium heat, stirring to help the sugar
    dissolve. Bring to the boil and continue boiling
    steadily, without stirring, until the sugar begins to
    darken and reaches light caramel stage (temperature
    340°F/ 171°C).

3. Remove from the heat at once, and stand the
    saucepan in cold water. Add the lemon juice and nuts
    and stir through the syrup. Turn the mixture onto a
    greased board and, with wet hands, shape small
    portions of it into uneven balls or mounds. Leave to
    get completely cold.

ALMOND HALVAH (Greece)

4 oz (115g) blanched almonds
Just under ½ pint (285ml) milk
6 oz (170g) raw cane sugar
Bare 1 oz (30g) butter

1. Grind the nuts to a powder in a blender, or with mortar and pestle. (You can use ready-ground nuts, but the flavour will not be as rich as if you grind your own.)

2. In a saucepan combine the ground almonds with the milk, bring to the boil, then continue boiling gently for about 10 minutes, until the mixture begins to thicken.

3. Still over the heat, add the sugar and stir until it dissolves. Add the butter and stir so that it is completely absorbed by the other ingredients.

4. When thick and paste-like, remove the mixture from the heat and pour into a shallow greased tin, spreading it evenly. Leave to cool then cut into squares.

WHOLESOME
AND DELICIOUS

CAROB RAISIN CLUSTERS

4 oz (115g) plain carob 'chocolate' bar
4 oz (115g) raisins

1. Break the bar into small pieces, and melt it gently either in the top of a double boiler, or in a bowl suspended over a pan of hot water (take care the bowl does not actually touch the water). Cover the bowl, and stir occasionally.

2. Remove from the heat and cool for a minute or two, then drop the raisins into the sauce and stir them well.

3. Using a metal spoon, lift them out a few at a time, and drop into small mounds on wax paper, leaving space between them, or in individual paper cases. Allow to harden completely before serving or storing.

CARROT BALLS

½ lb (225g) raw cane sugar
Bare 4 tablespoonsful water
1 lb (455g) finely grated carrots
Squeeze of lemon juice
1 oz (30g) pistachio nuts or almonds
Extra nuts or sugar for coating

1. In a heavy saucepan, and over a low heat, dissolve the sugar in two tablespoonsful of the water. Add the grated carrot and cook gently, without stirring, until the carrots are soft.

2. Add the rest of the water and the lemon juice, and continue cooking until the mixture thickens to a paste. Stir in the coarsely crushed nuts.

3. Turn the mixture onto a lightly greased tray and leave to cool for a few minutes. Then, with wet hands, divide the paste into small balls and coat each one with more nuts or sugar. Set aside to get cold before serving.

'LIQUORICE' BITES

2 oz (55g) powdered milk
2 oz (55g) wheatgerm
1 good tablespoonful molasses
1 teaspoonful vanilla essence
Approx. 2 tablespoonsful water

1. In a bowl stir together the sifted milk powder and wheatgerm. Add the molasses and vanilla essence, working them into the dry ingredients to make a thick dough (this is easiest if you use your fingertips to rub the ingredients together). Add water as necessary.

2. Divide the mixture, then roll it into small balls and flatten them slightly. Set aside for a short while to firm up.

SOYA SESAME SWEETS

3 oz (85g) candied peel
2 oz (55g) sesame seeds
2 oz (55g) soya flour
1-2 tablespoonsful honey
Pinch of mixed spice

1. Chop the peel as fine as possible, and combine it with the sesame seeds and soya flour.

2. Stir in enough honey to hold the other ingredients

together, and flavour with a little mixed spice.

3. Use your hands to roll the mixture into small balls —
   if it seems too sticky, add more soya flour; if too dry
   add more honey. Arrange on a plate and set aside to
   firm up.

GRANOLA WALNUT BALLS

4 oz (115g) butter or polyunsaturated margarine
½ lb (225g) chopped dates
Good pinch of mixed spice
4 oz (115g) walnuts, chopped
3 oz (85g) granola cereal
Desiccated coconut to coat

1. In a heavy saucepan melt the fat, then stir in the finely
   chopped dates and spice. Cook gently, stirring
   frequently, until the ingredients blend to form a thick
   paste. Set aside to cool.

2. Stir in the chopped nuts and granola, mixing well,
   then roll the mixture into small balls. Coat each one
   with some of the coconut, and chill briefly to firm up.

FROSTED FRUIT

*Approx. ½ lb (225g) of fresh fruit: grapes, cherries,
    strawberries, tangerines**
1-2 egg whites
*Approx. 2 oz (55g) raw cane sugar, powdered in
    grinder*

1. First prepare the fruit. Wash and thoroughly dry the grapes, leaving them in small bunches of 3 or 4. If using cherries or strawberries, wash and pat them dry, leaving the stalks in place. Peel and break the tangerines into segments.

2. Whip the egg whites until just beginning to stiffen. Dip each piece of fruit into the egg white, then into the powdered sugar to make a light dusting that stays in place.

3. Put the fruit onto a wire rack and leave to dry in a warm room for several hours. Arrange on an attractive dish before serving.

*Use one kind of fruit only, or a combination. This is a particularly pretty way to serve fruit, so choose the colours and variety of fruit with their appearance very much in mind.

ORANGE AND APRICOT SLICES

5 oz (140g) dried apricots, soaked for a short time
1½ oz (45g) desiccated coconut
1 tablespoonful finely grated orange peel
1 tablespoonful concentrated orange juice

1. Drain the apricots, pressing them well to remove all the moisture, then chop or mince them to make a coarse paste. (If they are rather rough, cook them briefly first.)

2. Stir in most of the coconut, the orange peel and juice, and mix thoroughly.

3. Divide the paste into two, roll into small sausage shapes, and coat with the extra desiccated coconut. Wrap each roll in clingfilm and chill well before cutting into slices and serving.

MOLASSES TOFFEE APPLES

4 medium eating apples
½ lb (225g) raw cane sugar
4 oz (115g) molasses
2 oz (55g) butter or polyunsaturated margarine
Good teaspoonful vinegar

1. Wipe the apples to ensure that they are clean, and if the skins are extra shiny, use a sharp knife or fine grater to roughen them a little. Remove the stalks.

2. In a large saucepan combine the sugar, molasses, fat and vinegar. Over a medium heat, bring the mixture to the boil, stirring continually to make sure the sugar has dissolved. Continue boiling for about 20 minutes until it reaches hard crack stage (temperature 310°F/154°C). Remove from the heat at once.

3. Spear each apple with a stick. Dip them one at a time into the toffee, turning them so that the apples are completely and evenly coated. Leave to cool on a greased tray, or standing in a jam jar.

FRUIT AND NUT TRUFFLES

5 oz (140g) prunes
5 oz (140g) dates
10 oz (285g) raisins
3 oz (85g) desiccated coconut
2 oz (55g) wheatgerm
1-2 tablespoonsful honey
1-2 tablespoonsful concentrated orange juice
1-2 tablespoonsful grated orange peel

1. Remove stones from the prunes, clean the fruit, then mince or chop it as fine as possible. Mix with most of the coconut, and all of the wheatgerm, making sure the ingredients are evenly distributed.

2. Stir in enough honey and fruit juice to make a thick paste. Adjust the consistency with more juice if necessary, or more wheatgerm if it seems too soft. Add the orange peel to taste.

3. Shape the mixture into small balls and roll them in the rest of the coconut. Put each one in a small paper case and leave for a few hours, preferably overnight, to firm up. If the truffles are not to be eaten at once, store covered in the fridge.

QUINCE SQUARES

2 lb (1.15 kilos) quinces
Approx. 1½ lbs (680g) raw cane sugar
1 tablespoonful finely grated lemon rind
Good pinch ground cinnamon

1. Wash the quinces and remove the cores, then cut into small pieces. Steam them until tender, then cool slightly.

2. Make a purée by forcing the fruit through a fine sieve or colander. Discard the peel and any pips that are left behind.

3. Weigh the purée, then put it into a saucepan with an equal weight of sugar. Simmer the mixture, stirring continually, until it thickens and comes away from the sides of the pan. Add the lemon rind and cinnamon.

4. Lightly butter a shallow tin and pour in the prepared mixture, spreading it evenly. Put into a very cool oven (temperature 250°F/ 130°C — Gas Mark ½) for a short time to harden the purée. Cut into 1 in. (2cm) squares when cool.

Note: Other fruits can be treated in the same way. Ground or chopped nuts can be added.

PISTACHIO STUFFED APRICOTS

1 lb (455g) whole dried apricots
3 oz (85g) pistachio nuts
3 oz (85g) ground almonds
Approx. 2 oz (55g) raw cane sugar, powdered in
    grinder
A little concentrated orange juice or
    1 egg white

1. Soak the apricots overnight, then cook on a very low
    heat until just tender. Drain well, taking care not to
    break them.

2. Mix together the pistachio nuts, ground almonds and
    most of the sugar. Use the fruit juice or egg white to
    bind the ingredients together.

3. Fill each of the apricots with some of the mixture,
    mould the fruit back into shape, and roll each one in
    the remaining sugar. Leave to dry on a wire rack
    before serving.

DRIED FRUIT CHOCOLATE BARS

4 oz (115g) prunes
4 oz (115g) apricots
4 oz (115g) dates
4 oz (115g) roasted hazelnuts
1 egg white
2 oz (55g) raw cane sugar chocolate

1. Wipe the fruit to make sure it is clean, remove the stones from the prunes, then mince or chop as finely as possible. Coarsely chop the nuts.

2. Use a little lightly beaten egg white to bind the ingredients together, then press them down into a small shallow tin that has been lined with greaseproof paper.

3. Break the chocolate and put it into the top of a double boiler, or a bowl suspended over a pan of hot water (making sure it does not actually touch the water). Cover, and stir every now and again until the chocolate melts to form a thick sauce.

4. Use a knife to spread the chocolate over the dried fruit and nut mixture. Leave to set. Cut into bars.

CHERRY NUT BALLS

4 oz (115g) blanched almonds
4 oz (115g) skinned hazelnuts
½ lb (225g) raw cane sugar, powdered in grinder
1-2 egg whites
Glace cherries*

1. Grind the almonds and hazelnuts to a fine powder, and mix well with the powdered sugar.

2. Add enough lightly beaten egg white to make a thick paste, and knead this lightly for a minute or two so that it is completely smooth.

3. Wipe any excess syrup from the cherries. Divide the nut paste into small pieces of an equal size, and wrap each one around a cherry, making a ball. Leave them on a wire rack for a few hours to harden. If not for immediate consumption, store in an airtight tin.

Other fillings can be used for these sweets. Try a piece of candied peel, dried apricot or pear, or a whole nut.

TAHINI SLICES

3 tablespoonsful tahini
3 tablespoonsful honey
3 oz (85g) ground sunflower seeds
2 oz (55g) desiccated coconut
1 oz (30g) wheatgerm or bran
4 oz (115g) raisins

1. Mix the tahini and honey together, then stir in the other ingredients to make a fairly firm dough. Adjust the consistency if it isn't quite right — add more sunflower meal, coconut or wheatgerm to make it more dry, or more tahini if it needs to be softened.

2. Separate the dough into two portions and shape them into rolls. Wrap in clingfilm and chill in the fridge, then serve cut into fairly thick slices.

CLIVE BIRCH

FIG CAKES

½ lb (225g) dried figs
3 oz (85g) unblanched almonds
1-2 tablespoonsful ground cinnamon
1 teaspoonful ground fennel
Rice paper (optional)
Raw cane sugar (optional)

1. Mince the figs, or chop them as finely as possible, and put into a bowl. Add the coarsely chopped almonds and spices, and use a wooden spoon to mix well together, pressing the figs against the sides of the bowl to make a paste.

2. Shape portions of the mixture into balls, then flatten them gently to make into round cakes. Set aside to firm up. If you prefer, flatten the fig mixture between sheets of rice paper and trim round the cakes; or coat them in sugar, press down so that it stays in place, and leave for a short time so that the sugar flavour is absorbed by the mixture.

NIBBLERS' DELIGHTS

SWEET PEANUT POPCORN

Approx. 1 tablespoonful vegetable oil
2 oz (55g) popping corn
1 oz (30g) raw cane sugar
1 oz (30g) roasted peanuts, coarsely chopped

1. Coat the base of a large saucepan with the oil, then add the corn and sugar, and cover with a well-fitting lid.

2. Place on a medium heat, shaking vigorously every now and again, and continue cooking until th popping stops.

3. Tip the mixture into a bowl straight away, and sti in the nuts. The popcorn can be eaten straight away or left to get cold.

SPICED PEAR GRANOLA

3 tablespoonsful vegetable oil
6 tablespoonsful honey
2 tablespoonsful lemon peel, finely chopped
Approx. 1 teaspoonful ground cinnamon
Approx. 1 teaspoonful mixed spice
1 lb (455g) rolled oats
3 oz (85g) cashew pieces
3 oz (85g) almonds
4 oz (115g) bran
3 oz (85g) desiccated coconut
3 oz (85g) sesame seeds
5 oz (140g) dried pears

1. Mix together the oil, honey, peel and spices. Combine
    all the dry ingredients except the pears, and spread
    them across one or two baking trays. Pour on the
    liquid mixture, stirring so that everything is well
    mixed.

2. Bake the granola uncovered in a low oven,
    temperature 225°F/110°C (Gas Mark ¼) for 45
    minutes to 1 hour, stirring frequently. The granola
    is ready when it is crisp and golden.

3. Remove from the heat , stir in the chopped pears, and
    leave to cool completely. Store in an airtight jar, and
    either nibble it just as it is, or serve with milk or fruit
    juice for breakfast, or as an any-time snack.

PEANUT CRISPS

2 oz (55g) peanuts
1 egg white
Approx. 4 oz (115g) raw cane sugar, powdered in grinder

1. Remove skins from the peanuts. If this is difficul roast them in the oven for a short time first.

2. Beat the egg white until just beginning to stiffen, the stir in enough powdered sugar to make a mixture th will coat a spoon.

3. Dip the nuts into the egg and sugar mixture, and pla on a baking sheet that has been covered wi greaseproof paper. Bake at 350°F/180°C (Gas Ma 4) for 5 minutes, or until the coating is light. browned. Leave to cool on the tray.

BRAZILIAN MUNCH

4 oz (115g) Brazil nuts
2 oz (55g) cashew pieces
2 oz (55g) banana chips
1 oz (30g) dried apples
1 oz (30g) preserved or candied pineapple
2 oz (55g) coconut flakes
4 oz (115g) granola

1. Chop the Brazil nuts into halves or large pieces (you can buy broken Brazil nuts, usually at a lower price than that charged for whole nuts, but make sure they are fresh).

2. Combine the Brazil pieces with all the other ingredients. Store in an airtight jar or tin and use as needed.

MEDITERRANEAN MIX

2 oz (55g) almonds
2 oz (55g) pine nuts
2 oz (55g) chopped dried peaches
2 oz (55g) dried cherries
2 oz (55g) chopped dried figs
4 oz (115g) raisins
2 oz (55g) roasted hazelnuts

1. Mix all the ingredients together and store in an airtight jar or tin for use as needed.

Note: Both the above mixes are only examples of the kind of combination you can make, using whatever ingredients you have to hand, and most enjoy eating. Remember to contrast dry and crunchy nuts with sweet fruits. Proportions can also be changed to suit your taste.

INDEX

Almond
    Halvah, 43
Almonds,
    Sugared, 34

Brazilian
    Munch, 61

Carob Raisin
    Clusters, 44
Carob Truffles,
    Creamy, 18
Carrot Balls, 45
Cherry Nut
    Balls, 55
Chocolate
    Brazils, 24
Coconut Barfi,
    33
Coffee Creams,
    22
Cranberry
    Sweets, 31

Edinburgh
    Rock, 20

Fig Cakes, 57
Fondant Roll, 16
Fruit and Nut
    Truffles, 51
Fruit Chocolate
    Bars, Dried,
    54
Fruit, Frosted,
    48

Ginger Tablet,
    Preserved, 13
Granola Walnut
    Balls, 47

Honey Noyeau,
    15

Lemon
    Lollipops, 25
Lime Peel,
    Candied, 37
Liquorice Bites,
    46

Maple Pecan
    Fondants, 40

Marrons Glacés,
    30
Marzipan Petits
    Fours, 26
Mediterranean
    Mix, 62
Molasses Toffee
    Apples, 50

Nougat, 28
Nougat with
    Nuts and
    Honey, 38

Orange and
    Apricot
    Slices, 49

Peanut Brittle,
    42
Peanut Crisps,
    60
Peanut Popcorn,
    Sweet, 58
Pear Granola,
    Spiced, 59

63

Pennies of Gold, 19

Peppermint Ice, 17

Pineapple Fudge, 23

Pine Nut Sweets, 36

Pistachio Ladus, 39

Pistachio Stuffed Apricots, 53

Quince Squares, 52

Sesame Crunch, 35

Soya Sesame Sweets, 46

Tahini Slices, Toffee, Angus 27
Everton, 21

Turkish Deligh 32

Yellow Man, 2

Yogurt Walnu Fudge, 14